A Feast of Saints

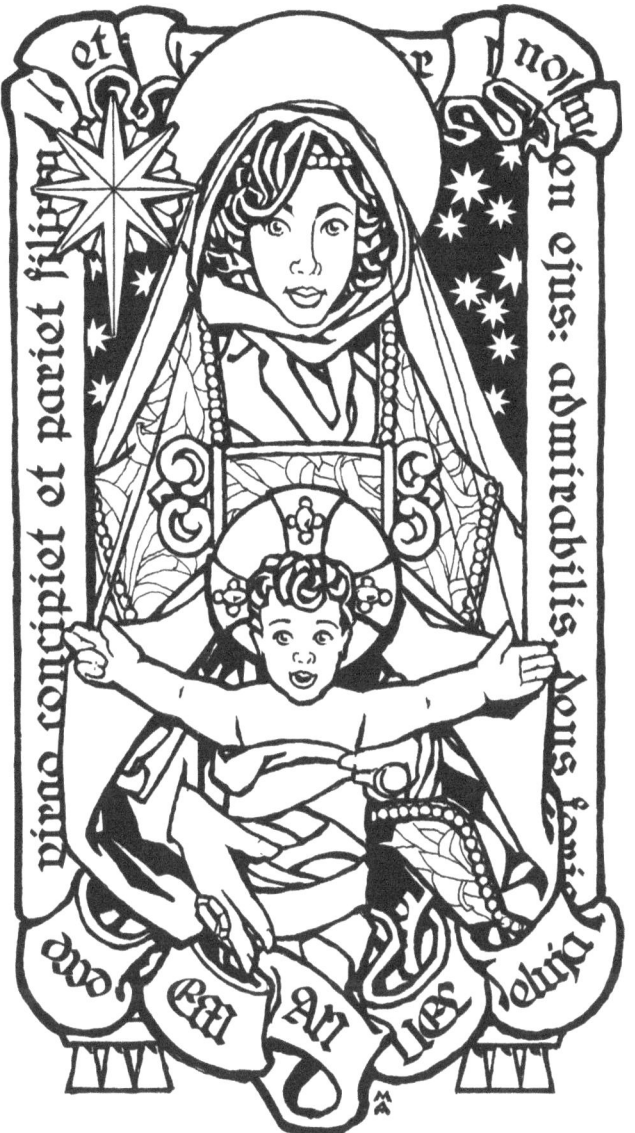

Matthew Alderman

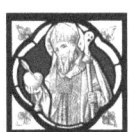

2016

ST. AUGUSTINE ACADEMY PRESS

HOMER GLEN, ILLINOIS

Copyright ©2016 by St. Augustine Academy Press. All illustrations ©2016 by Matthew Alderman. Used with permission.
All Rights Reserved. No part of this book may be reproduced or transmitted in any form or by any electronic or mechanical means, including photocopying, recording or by any information storage and retrieval systems, without permission in writing from Matthew Alderman.
Published in the U.S. by St. Augustine Academy Press, Homer Glen, Illinois.   ISBN 978-1-936639-79-3

St. Anthony was the son of a wealthy Portuguese nobleman. He joined the Franciscan Order and became a great preacher, even performing several miracles. He died at the age of 36 and was canonized just one year later. When his body was exhumed, his tongue was found to be incorrupt, in testimony to his great skill at preaching. He is shown in art holding the Christ Child, recalling a story told about a miraculous vision he had near Padua.

St. Patricia was a young noblewoman who is said to have been a descendant of Emperor Constantine. She fled to Rome to escape an arranged marriage, wishing to consecrate her virginity to Christ. There she received the veil from Pope Liberius. While on pilgrimage to Jerusalem, a terrible storm arose and she was shipwrecked near Naples. There she died shortly afterward, in approximately 665 AD. A vial of her blood is kept at a Monastery there bearing her name, and on Tuesday mornings and on her feast day, August 25, it is said to liquefy.

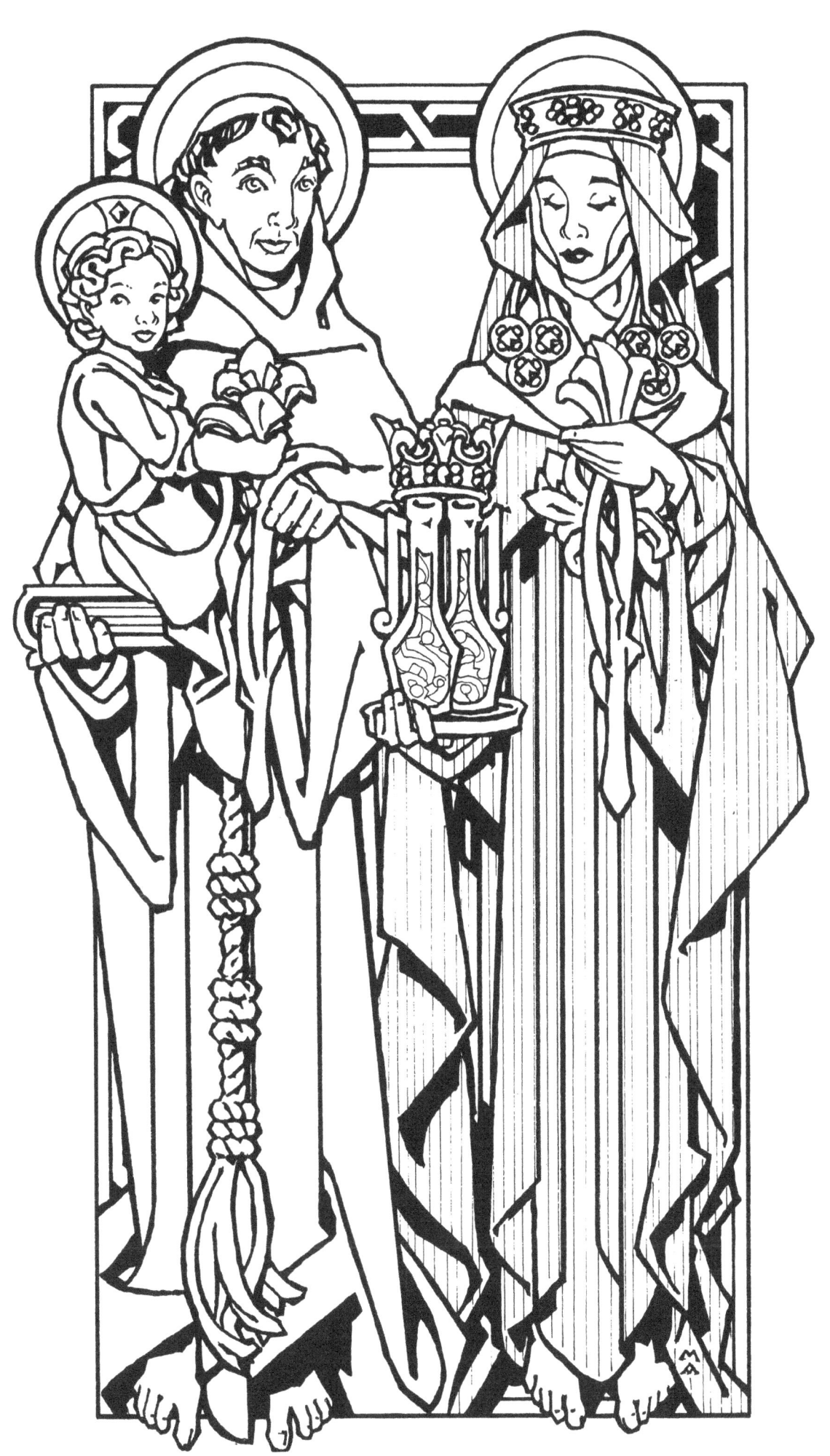

St. Lucy was a brave Christian maiden who lived during the 4th century. Having consecrated her virginity to God, she refused to marry the young man to whom her mother had betrothed her. Her angry suitor revenged himself by reporting her faith to the governor, and she suffered the death of a martyr in the year 303.
The palm she bears is a symbol of the victory of martyrdom.
She is a patron saint of the blind.

St. Odilia of Alsace was the daughter of a Frankish nobleman.
Born blind, her sight was miraculously restored when she was baptized.
She later founded the convent of Hohenburg on a mountaintop in Alsace
which now bears her name: Odilienberg, or Mont Sainte-Odile.

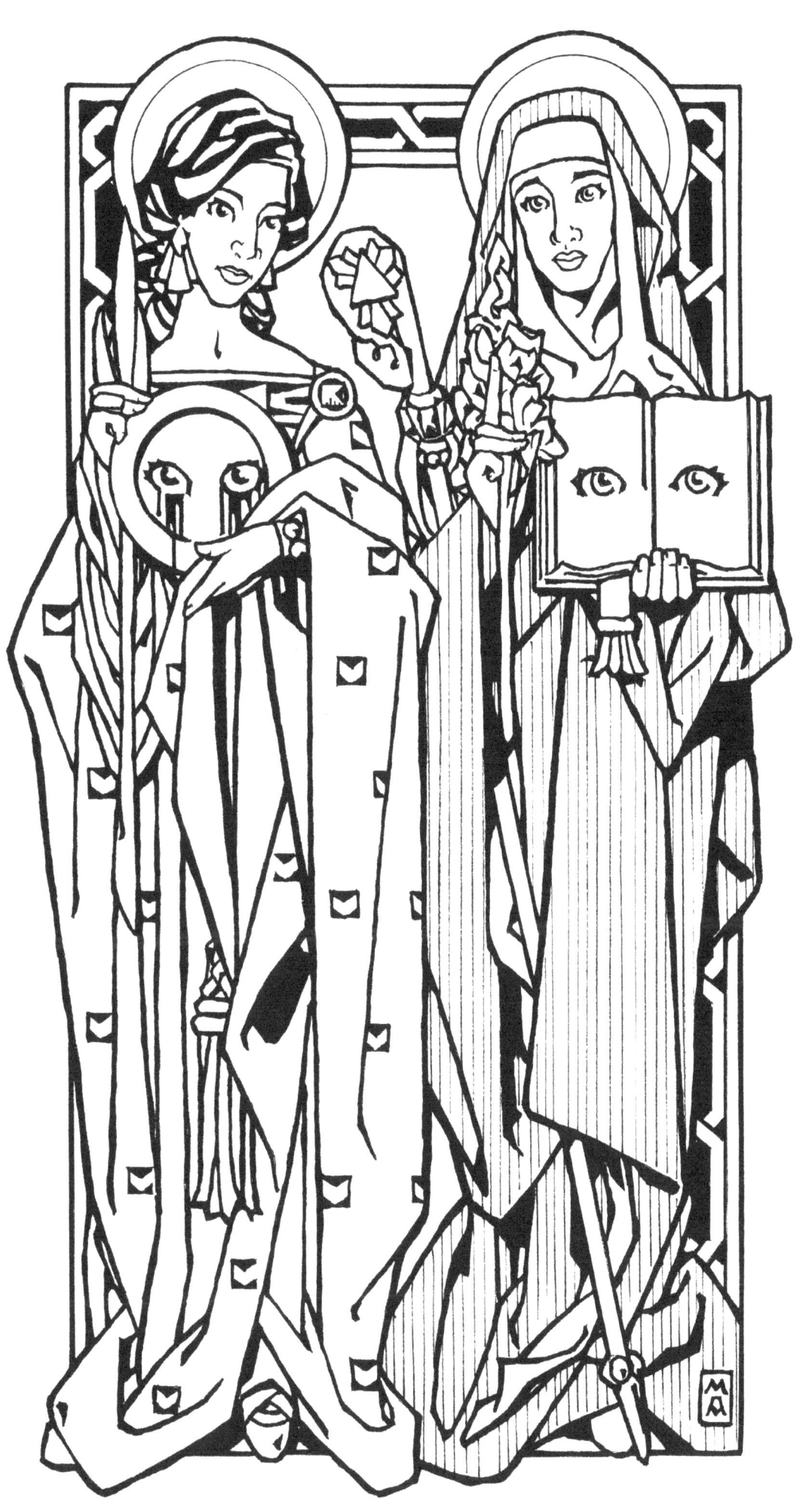

St. Barbara was raised in the 4th century by her father, who built a tower for her to live in, lest she come under the influence of others. When he learned of her conversion to Christianity, he denounced her before the tribunal and after she was tortured, he himself acted as her executioner. She is a patron saint invoked against sudden death, and so is sometimes also shown holding a chalice and host.

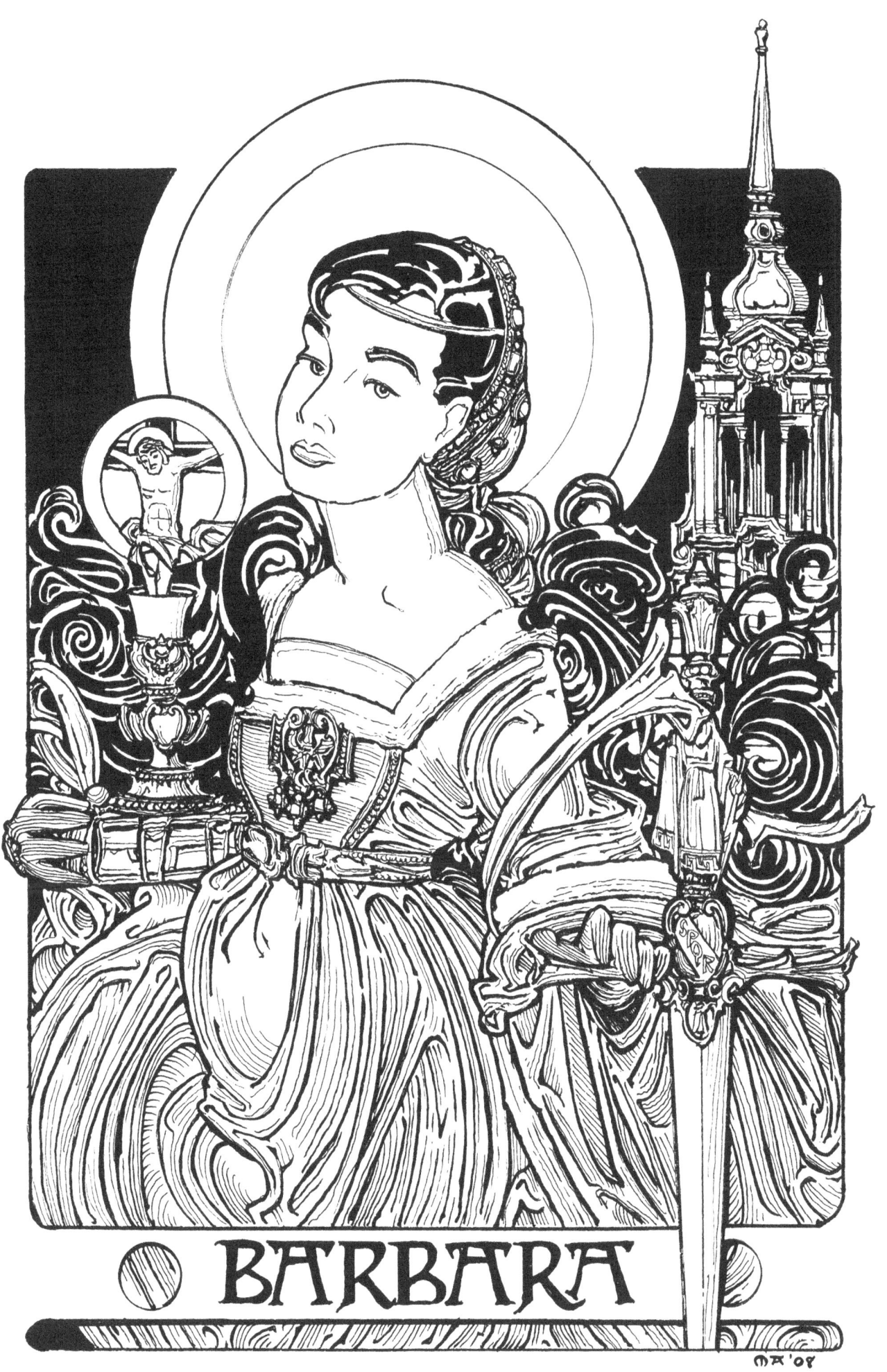

St. Catherine was born to a noble family in Alexandria and was known to be a great scholar. When she became a Christian due to a vision, she converted hundreds of others, even winning a debate against many of the best pagan philosophers of that time. Emperor Maxentius sought to convert her by torture, imprisonment and even by offering to marry her, but she refused and was condemned to die upon a spiked wheel. When it shattered at her touch, she was beheaded.

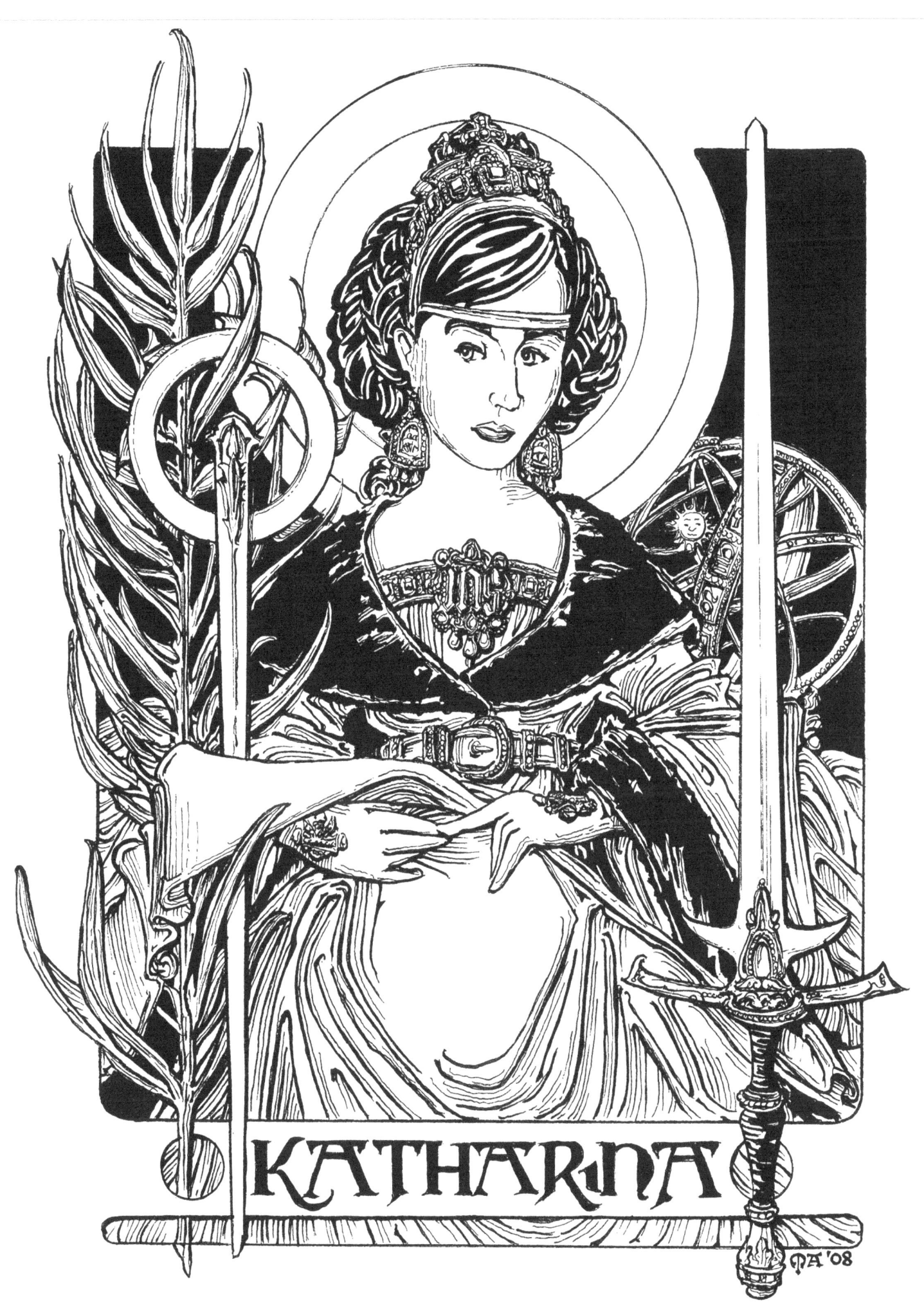

Saint Margaret of Antioch is an early Christian martyr about which little is known. Legend describes her as a young convert to Christianity who was disowned by her father, a pagan priest. She became a shepherdess, and, guarding her virginity, spurned the marriage proposal of a Roman governor, who had her put to death. One story says that during the course of her martyrdom, she was swallowed by a dragon, but escaped after making the sign of the Cross, which caused the beast to explode. She is one of the saints who spoke to Saint Joan of Arc in her visions.

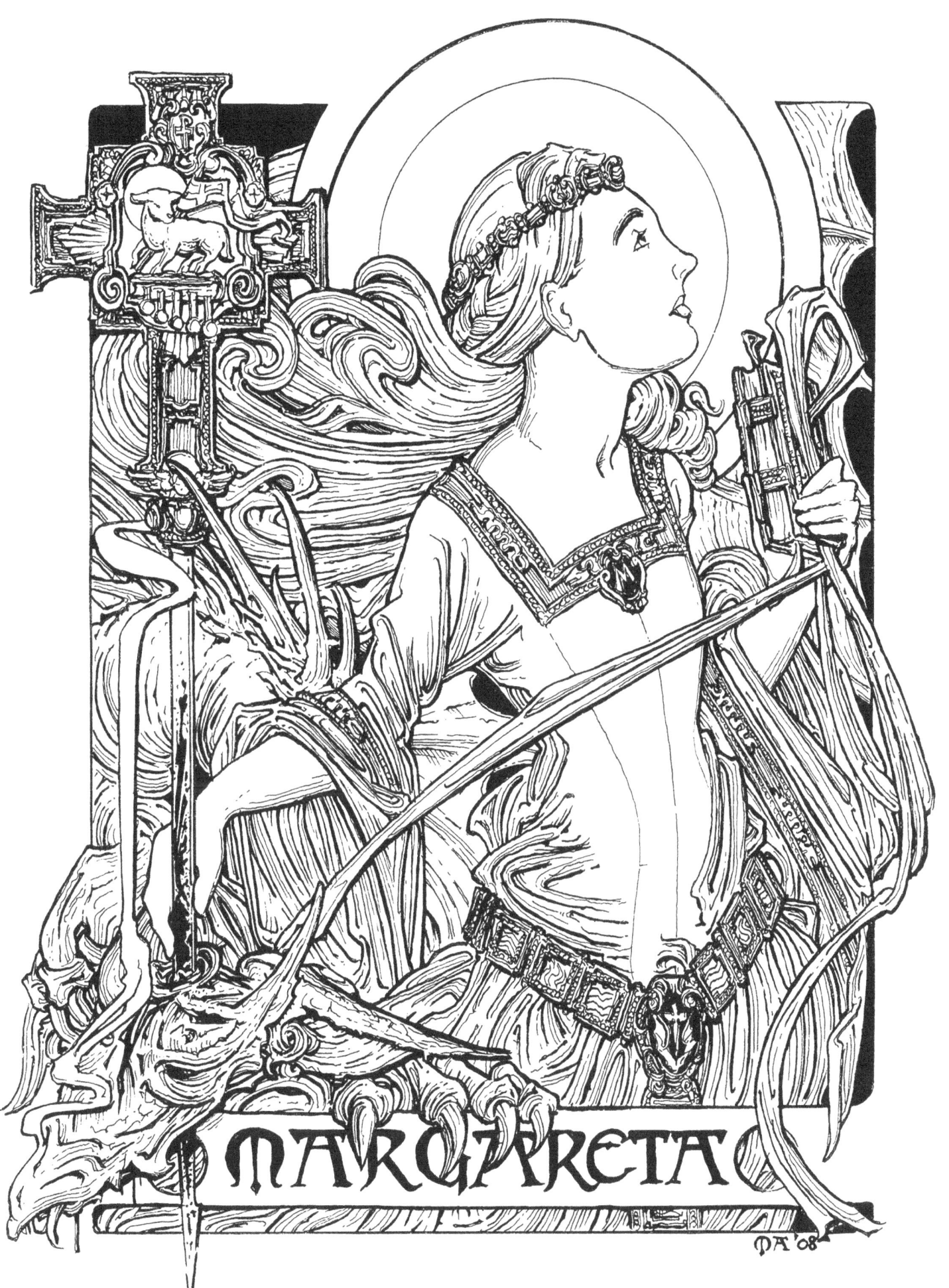

Very little is known about **St. Victoria** except for the fact that she was a virgin martyr who lived in Cordoba, Spain, and died in the year 304. She holds the arrows of her martyrdom, and a small image of her home city appears to the right of her face.

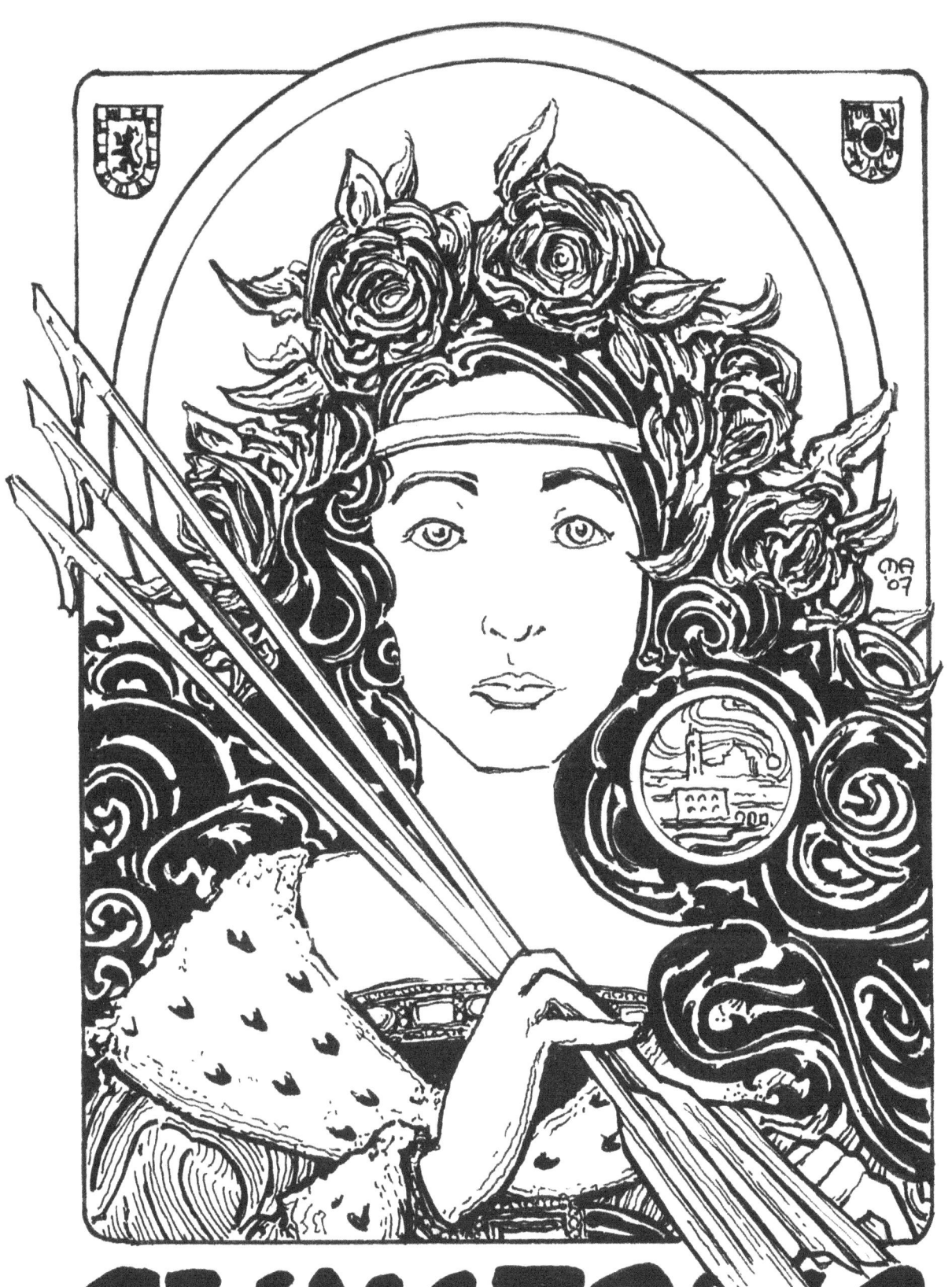

St. Philomena was unknown until her remains were discovered in 1802, and miracles came to be attributed to her relics. Among those saints who had a great devotion to her were St. John Vianney and St. Madeleine Sophie Barat. She is the only saint whose recognition is based solely on the basis of her powerful intercession, which have earned for her the title "wonder worker."

The many trials she suffered during her martyrdom are reflected in her emblems of sword, arrows and anchor; her miraculous rescue at one point during her passion is represented by the two angels. Her purity and the witness of her death are represented by red and white roses in her hair. A small image of her shrine in Mugnano, Italy, can be seen in lower right, and her status as the daughter of Greek royalty is represented by the ornamental patterns in the frame of the image.

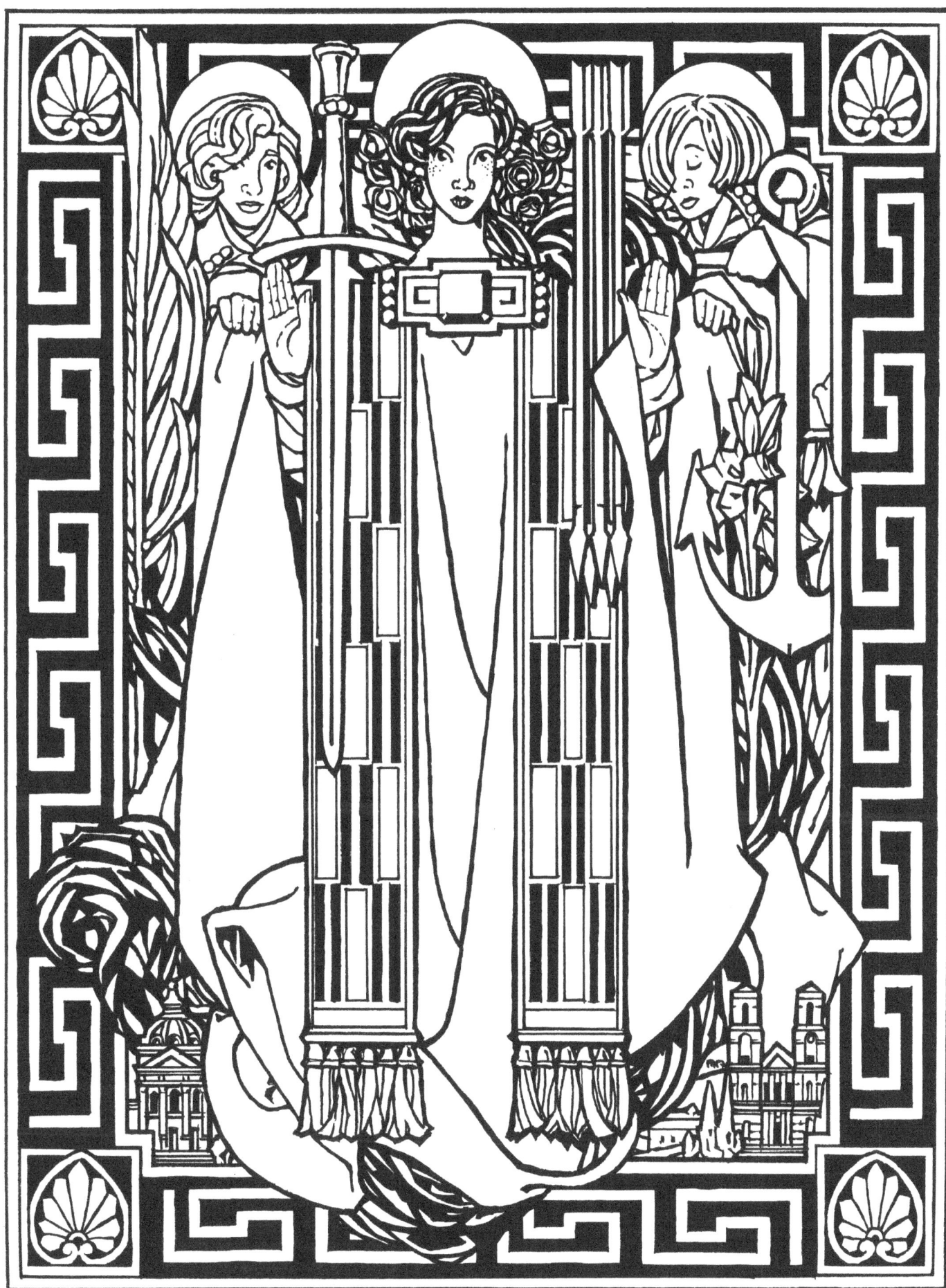

St. Margaret of Scotland was born in Hungary, where her father, the nephew of Edward the Confessor, was living in exile. After her father's death, she fled with her mother to Scotland, where she married King Malcolm III. Her virtuous example had a wonderfully civilizing influence upon her husband and his people, and together they served the poor and built many churches.

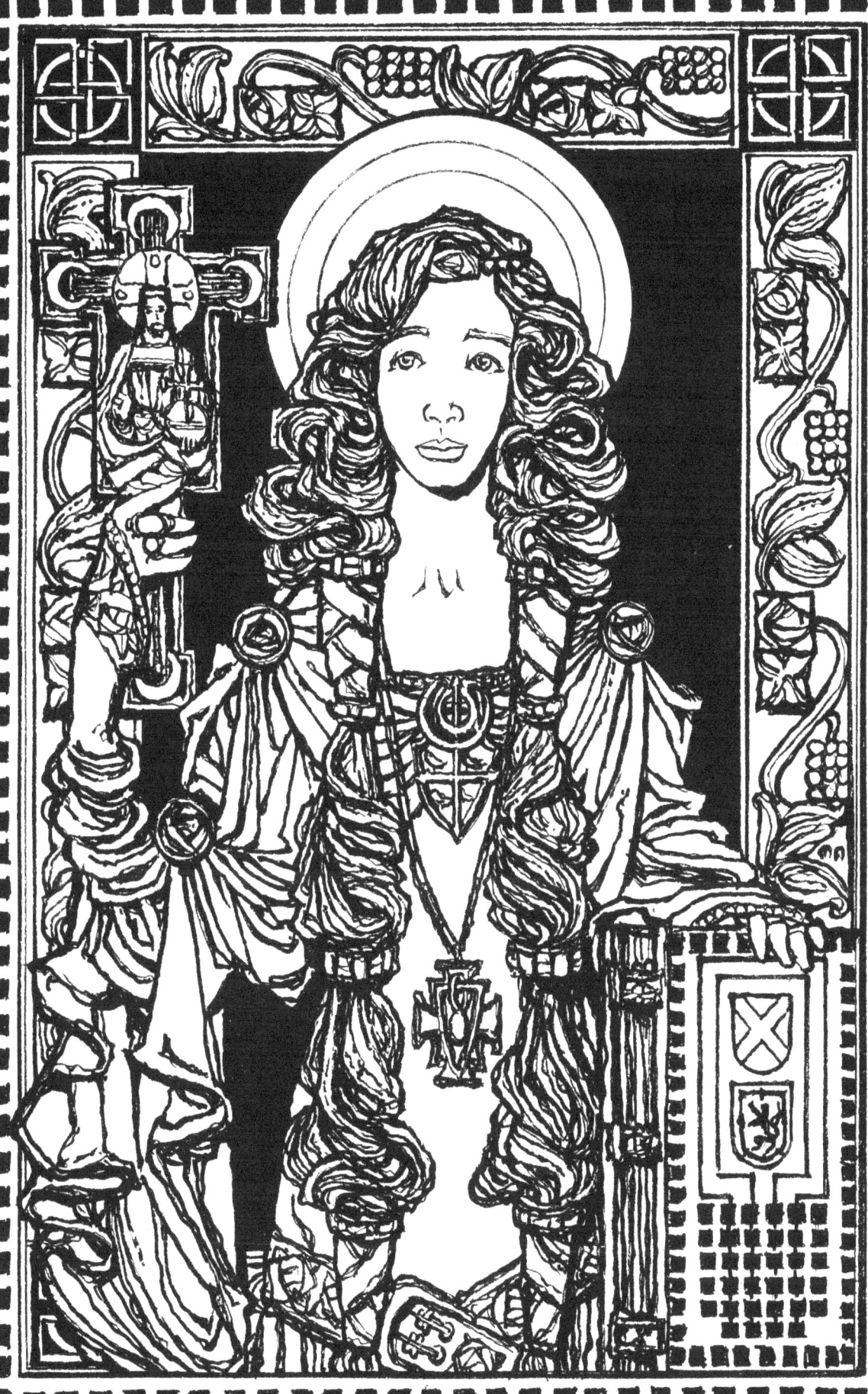

St. Bernard of Clairvaux was a virtuous young man who joined the Cistercian order
after his mother died. After founding the monastery of Clairvaux,
he was called upon to help settle the Papal Schism of 1130,
and then to combat the Cathars and other heresies.
Then Pope Eugene III commissioned him to preach the Second Crusade.
Though many were emboldened to fight due to his words, the Crusade was a failure,
and the responsibility for this overshadowed his later years.
In 1830, he was named a Doctor of the Church.

He is shown here flanked by two visions he experienced: one of these took place during
a serious illness, in which he saw the **Virgin Mary**
accompanied by **Sts. Lawrence and Benedict.**
The other was a vision of Christ revealing the wound He had received
from the pressure of the cross weighing on His shoulder.

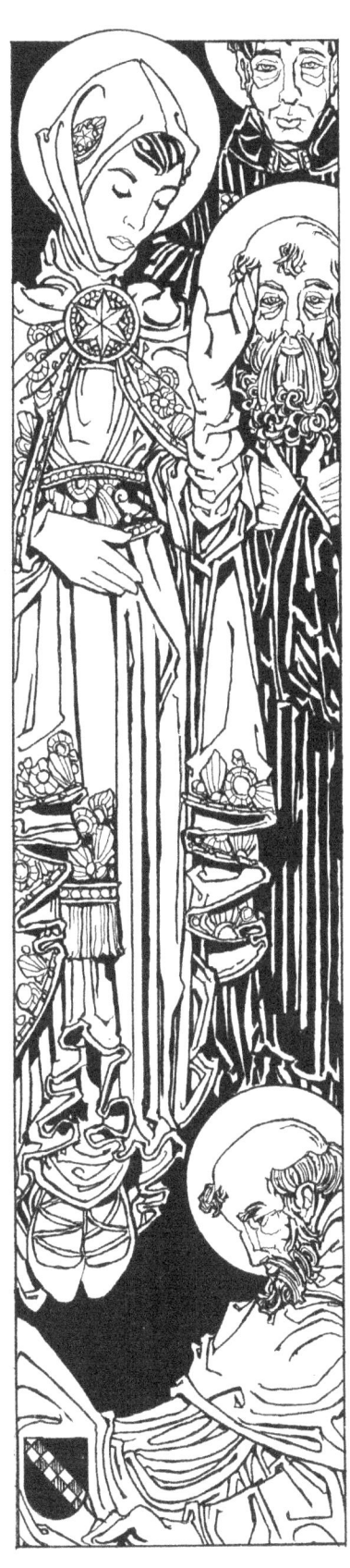
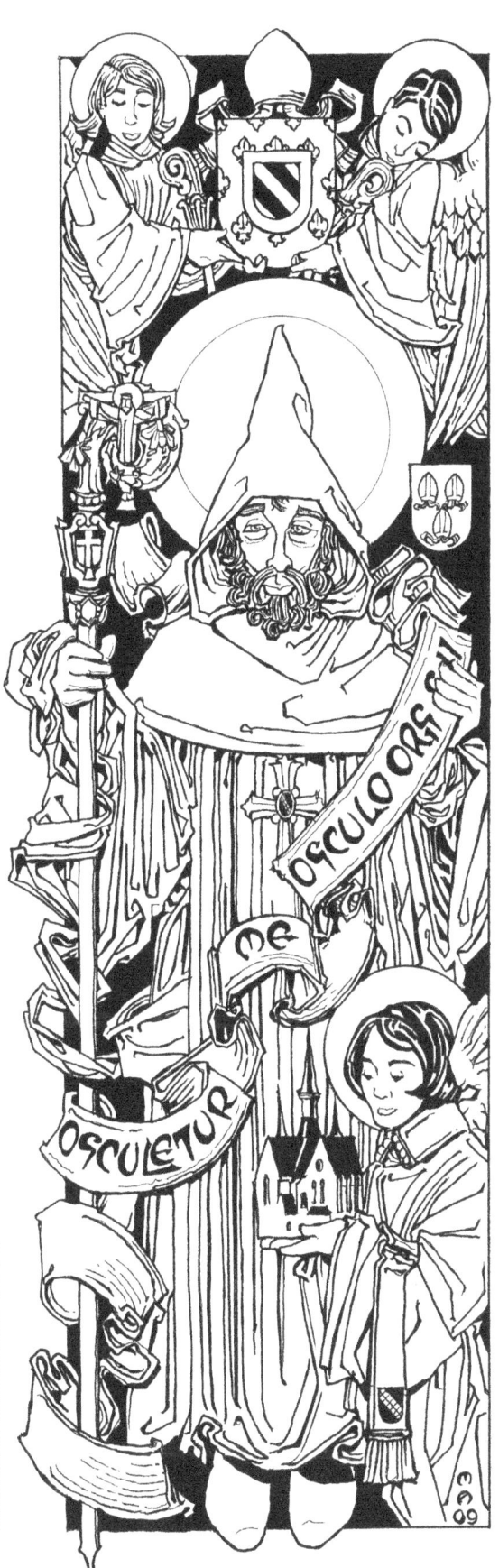
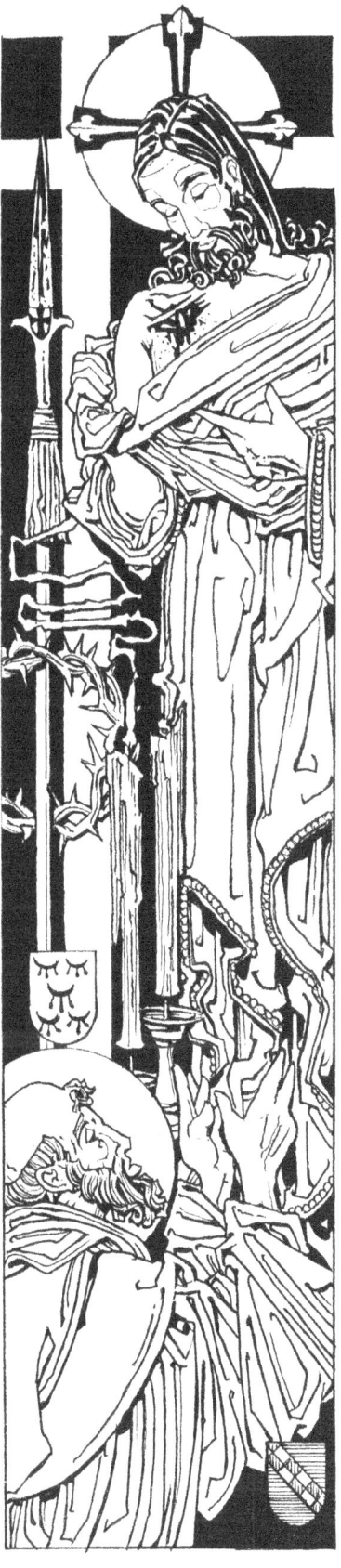

St. Cecilia was a young Christian noblewoman who was forced to marry a pagan. She converted him, his brother, and many of his friends, and all eventually gave their lives for their faith. When her time came to be sent to her death, she was condemned to be suffocated within the hot baths. When this failed to affect her, an executioner was sent to behead her but he failed in this task. She lived on for three days before dying.

Her guardian angel is shown to one side, while her husband and brother-in-law,
Sts. Valerian and Tiburtius, also martyrs, sit at her feet.
Symbols of church music surround her, for she is the patron saint of music.

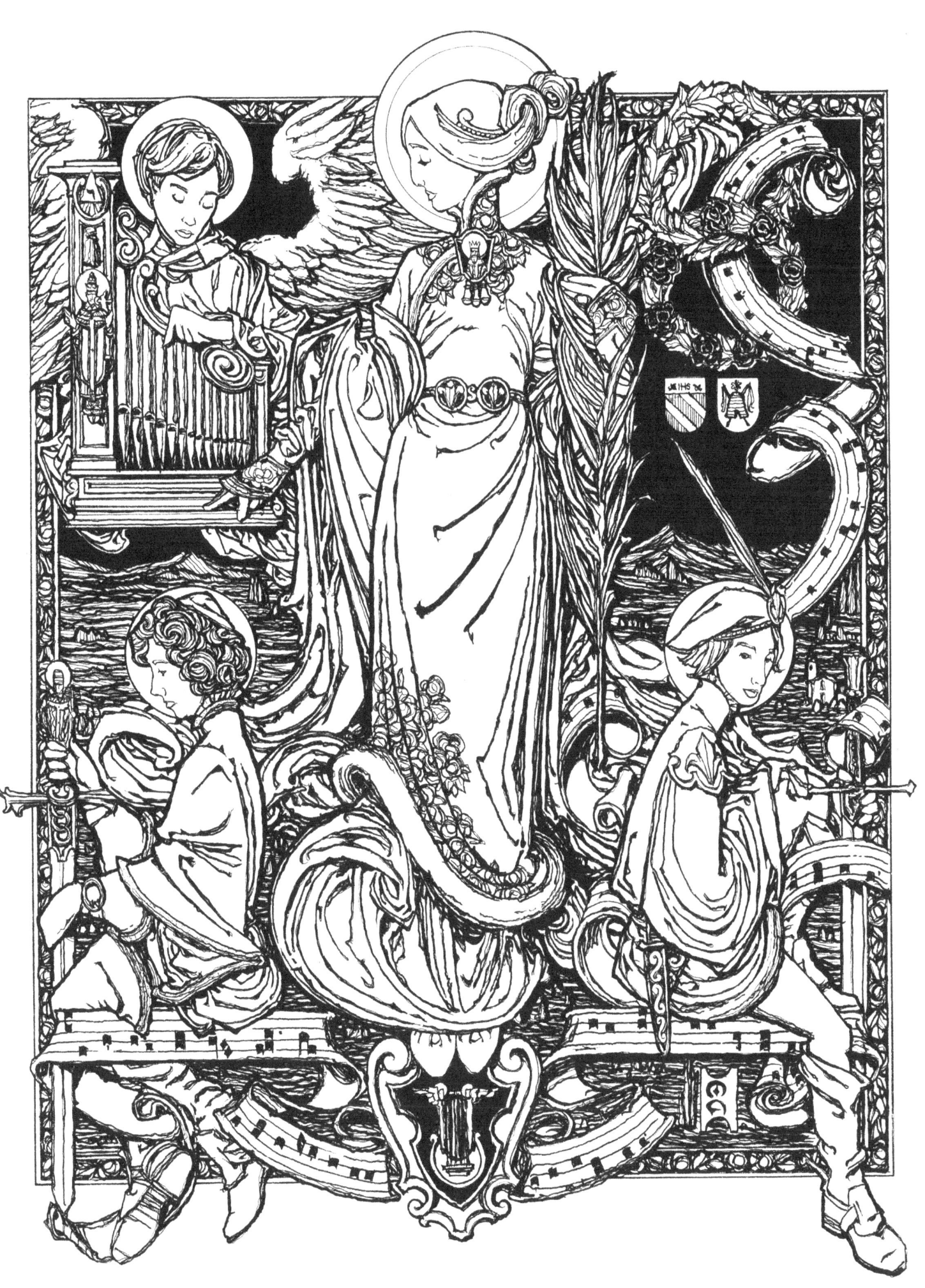

St. Augustine was the son of a Pagan father and a Christian mother. After a wild and dissipated youth, he embraced Christianity and was baptized by St. Ambrose. He then turned his great skills for speaking and writing toward the defense of the Faith. He became a bishop and one of the greatest saints and is one of the Doctors of the Church.

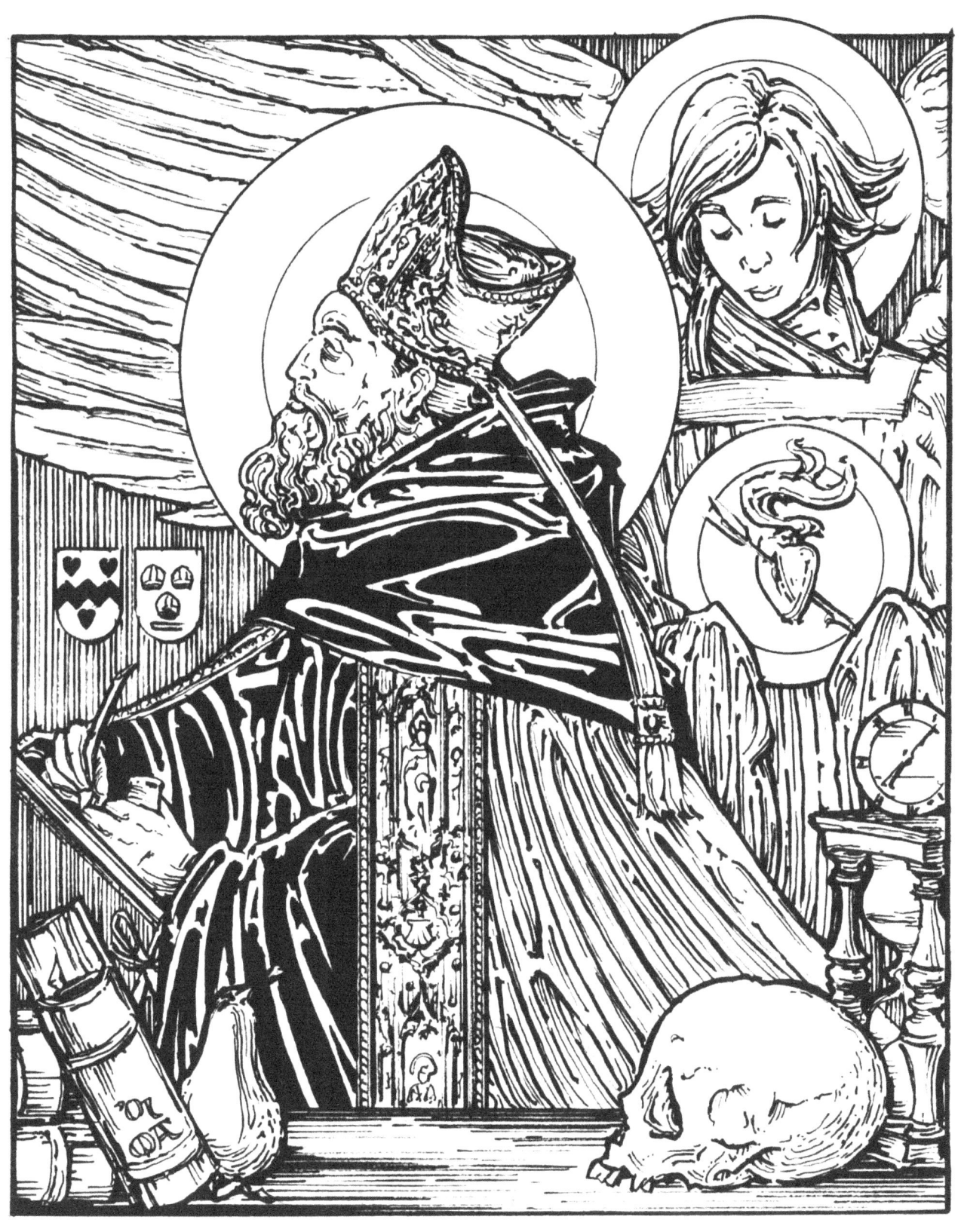

SQS · AUGUSTINUS

St. John Damascene lived in Syria in the 7th century, when it was in the hands of the Arabs. His father was one of the few Christians who had maintained a high office in the city. He was tutored by a wise monk and came to be highly respected even among the Saracens. He was an important figure in settling the Iconoclastic controversy, and wrote many hymns and prayers still used today in the Eastern Church.
He is a Doctor of the Church.

Recalling his defense of the use of images in the Church, he holds a representation of Our Lady under the title of "The Three-Handed Mother of God," which refers to a legend told about him in which his hand was miraculously restored.

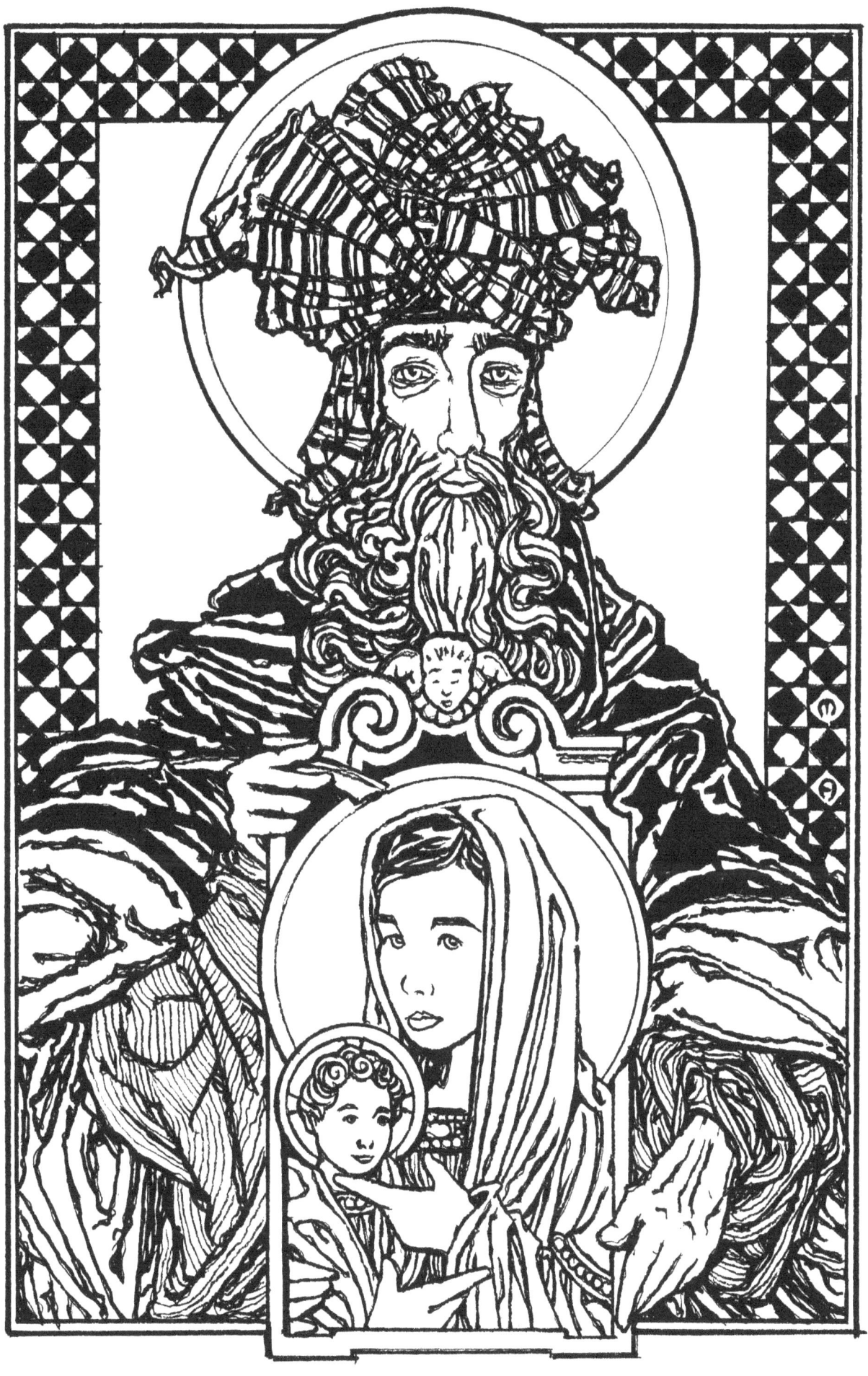

St. Dymphna was born in Ireland to a Pagan father and Christian mother. On the death of her mother, her father was urged to remarry, as his mental health began to rapidly decline. He swore to do so only if he could find a woman as beautiful as his wife. When such a woman proved difficult to find, his advisers suggested he might marry his 14-year-old daughter. In his madness, he embraced the idea, and Dymphna fled with the help of a priest. Her father found her in Belgium and when she refused to be his wife, he flew into a rage and beheaded her.
She is patron saint of those with mental illness.
She is shown here with the sword of her martyrdom, and trampling a devil.

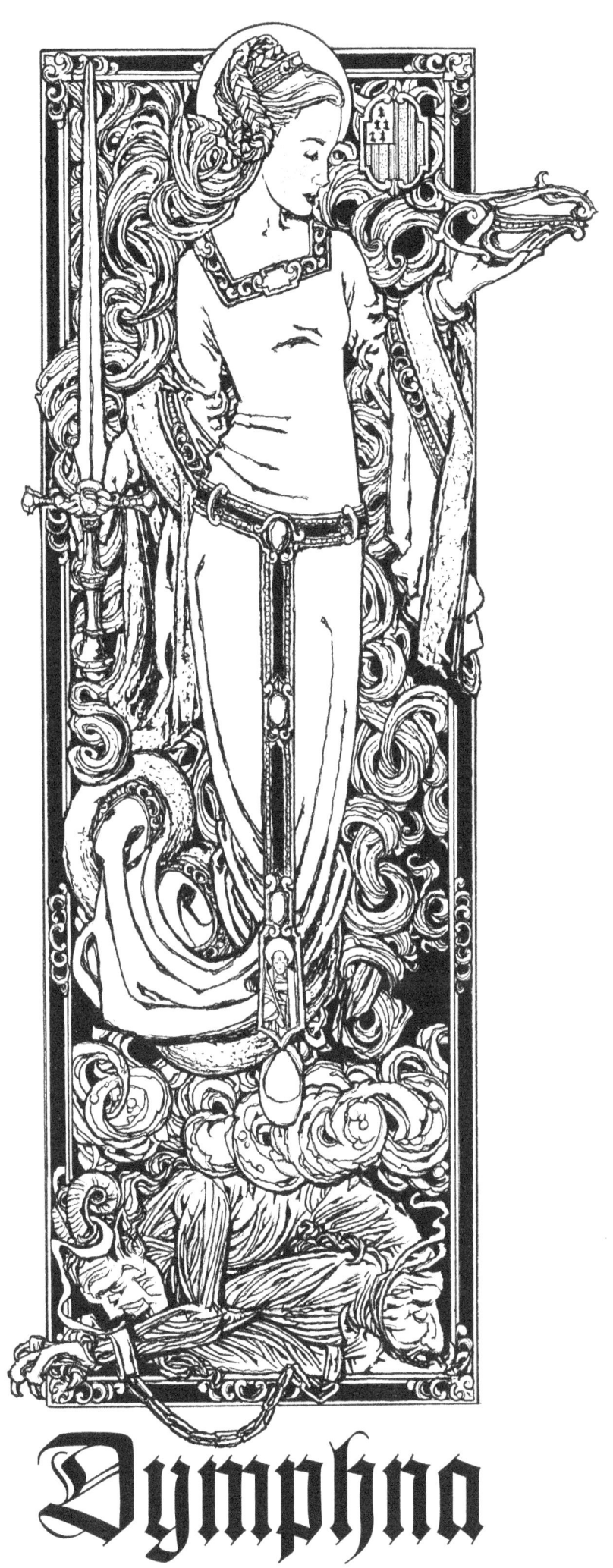

St. Josemaria was a Spanish priest and the founder of the Catholic organization Opus Dei. He believed that everyone could be called to holiness. He is shown here flanked by two angels, representing his great devotion to his guardian angel, and the fact that Opus Dei was founded on the feast-day of the Guardian Angel. This image is loosely inspired by a statue of him in the Vatican.

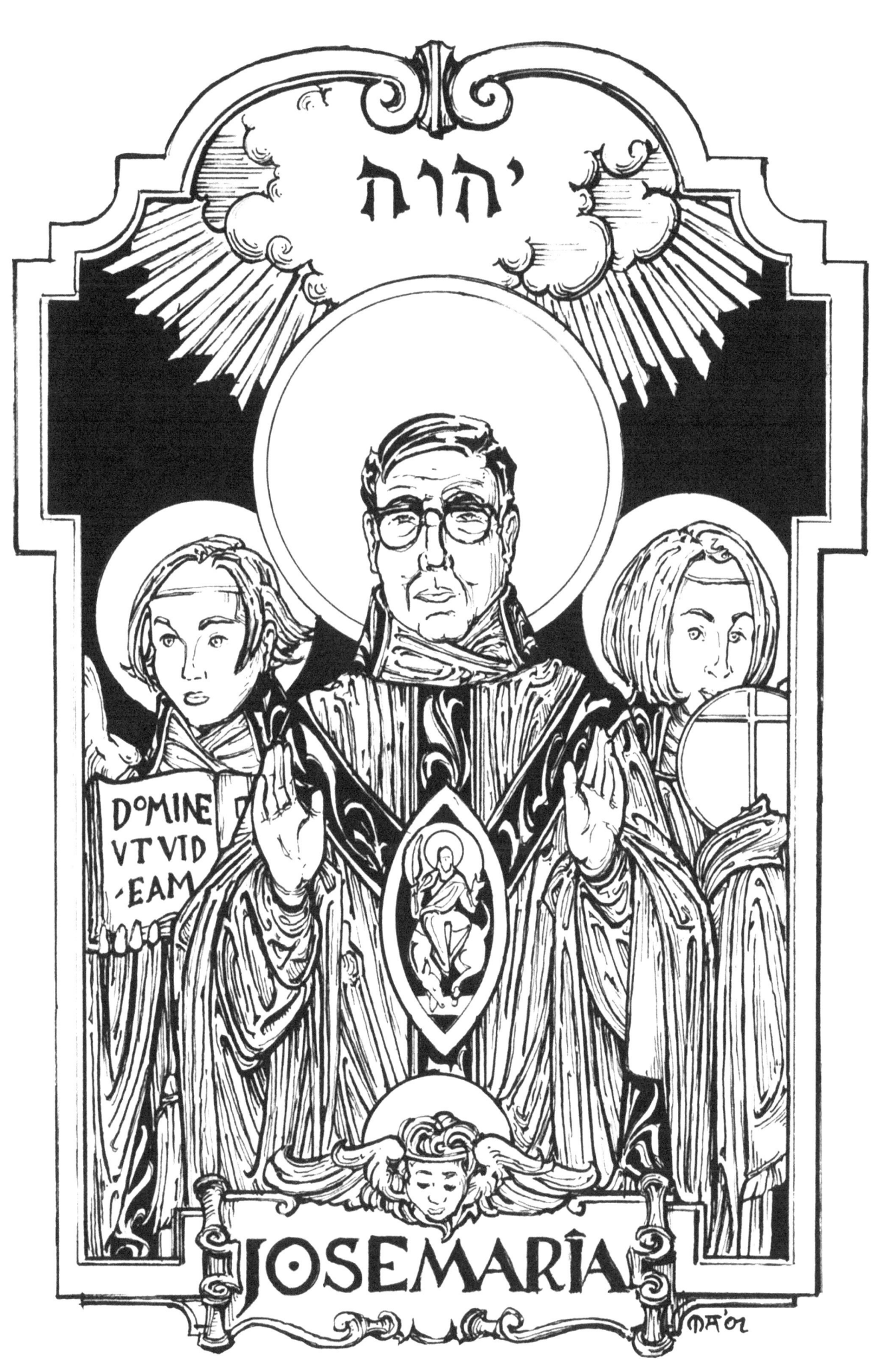

A story is told of **St. Anthony** that when he was at Rimini, he sought to convert the heretics there but they would not listen to him. Frustrated, he went to the seashore and called upon the fish to hear the Word of God. The fishes obeyed this command, listening attentively to him. When the people of the town saw what was happening, they too crowded the seashore and after listening to St. Anthony's eloquence, they renounced their heresy and were converted to the true faith. For constantly defending the truth of the Faith with his tongue, he is called the "Hammer of Heretics."

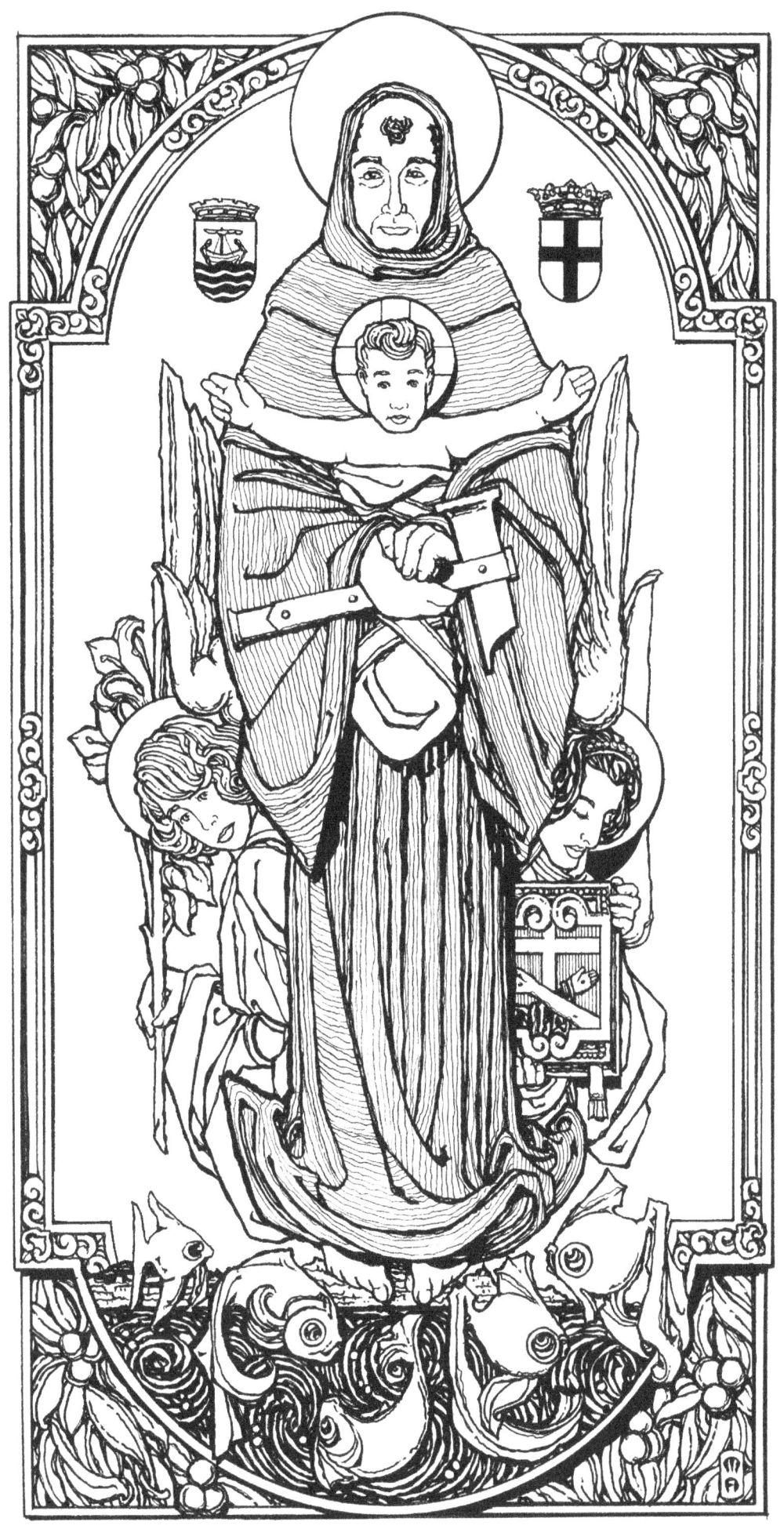

St. Agnes was a young Roman girl from a wealthy and pious family,
who rejected a pagan nobleman's offer of marriage. Denounced to the authorities
as a Christian, she was martyred by the sword in the year 304.
Her name sounds like the Latin word for lamb, *agnus*,
and this has since become a symbol for her purity.

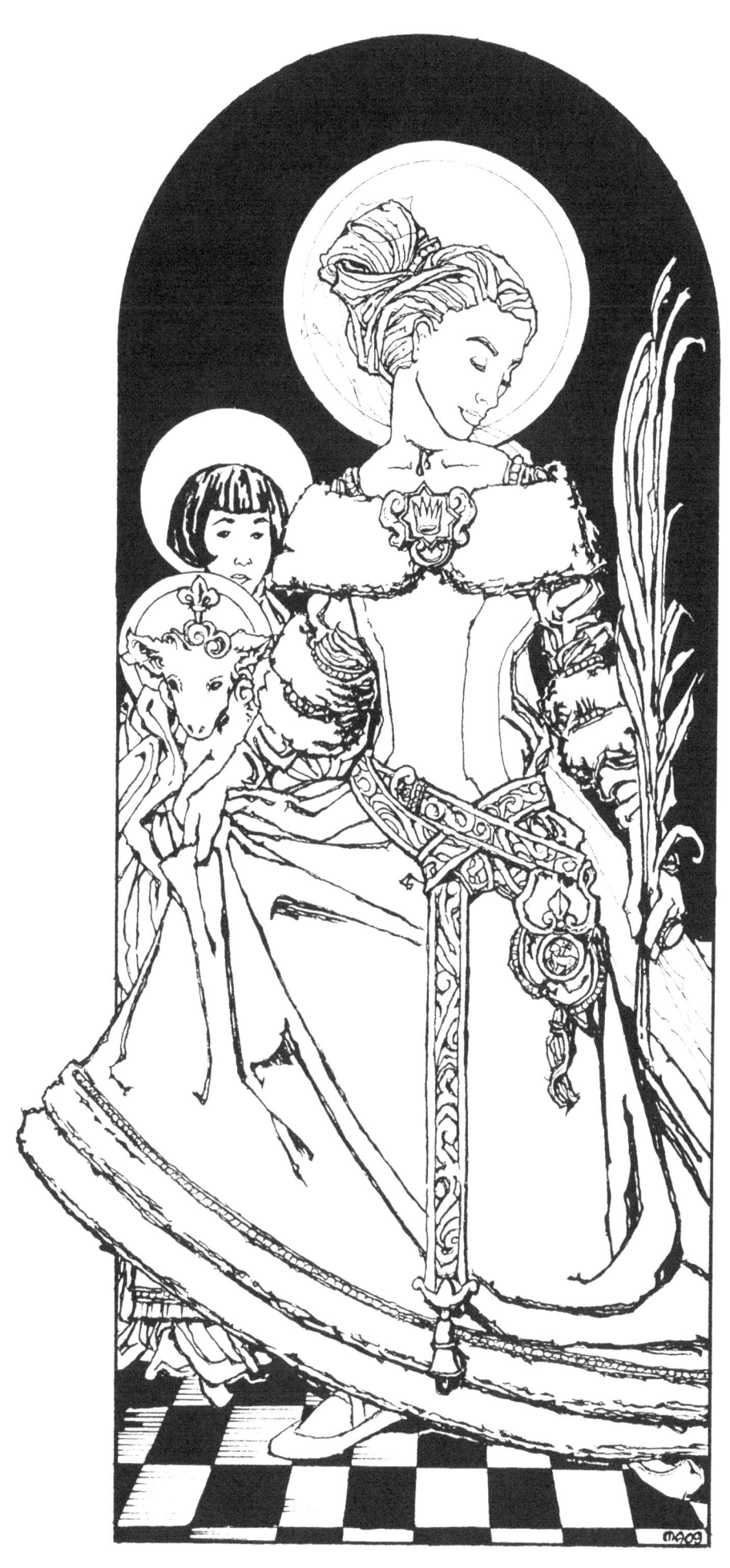

St. Stephen was the first Christian king of Hungary, crowned around the year 1000.
Under his rule, he founded many monasteries and churches,
defended the independence of his nation against the encroachments
of the Germans, and did much to spread Catholicism in his realm.
He is shown with a Hungarian double-barred cross, and the more ancient
national insignia of a shield with white and red stripes;
together, both are still used today by his homeland.
The crown he wears is based on a crown which still exists today—though
its connection with the saint is shrouded in legend—and which itself
has had a long and storied history.
His son, **Saint Emeric**, was greatly loved by him, though sadly,
he died young in a hunting accident.

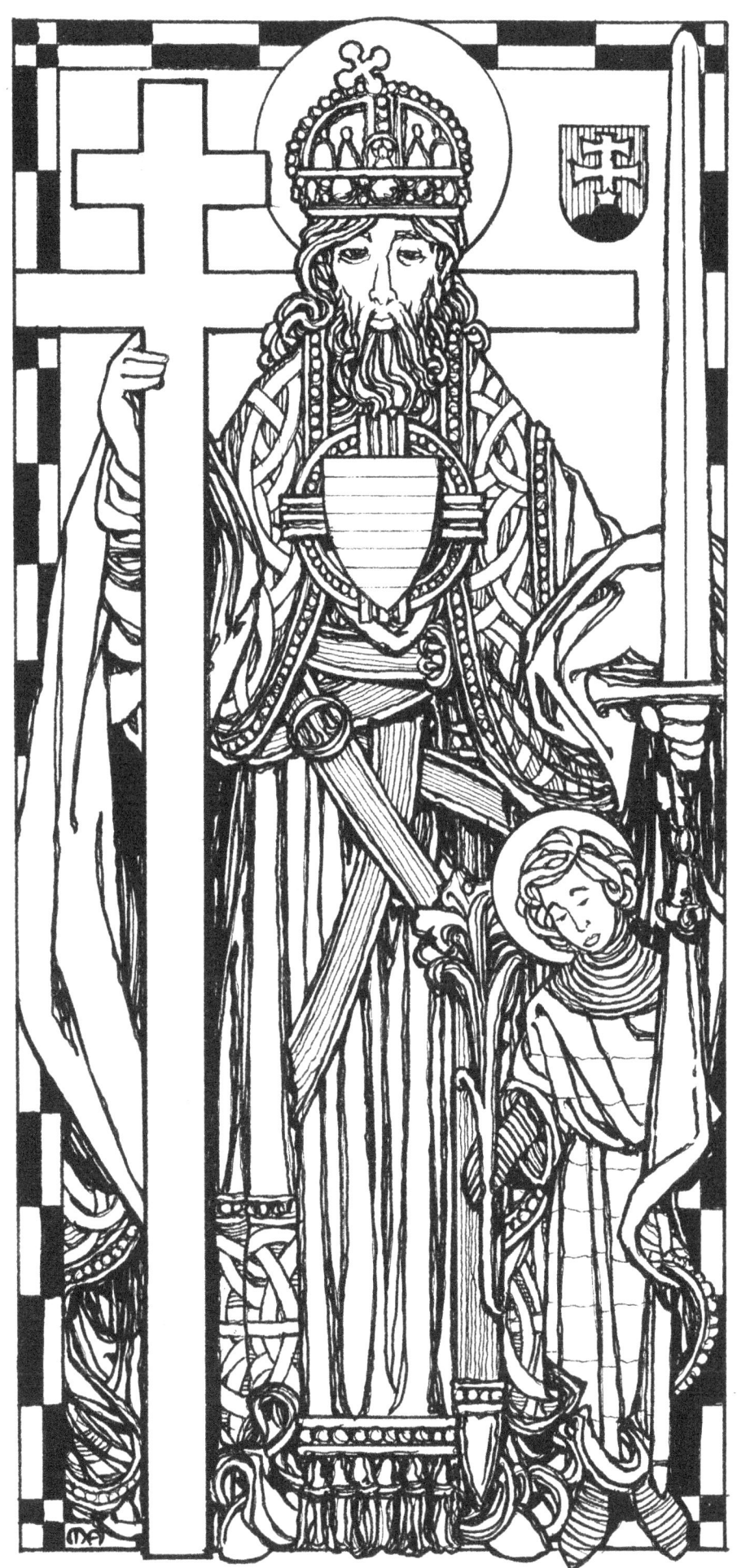

St. Matilda of Ringelheim was the wife of King Henry the Fowler of Germany. After he died, she and her son set up the convent of Quedlinburg, where her granddaughter was abbess. She is shown holding a model of the abbey, and the horse and eagle in the upper-right-hand corner symbolize her husband's royal status and her own bloodline as the daughter of a Saxon count in the region of Westphalia.

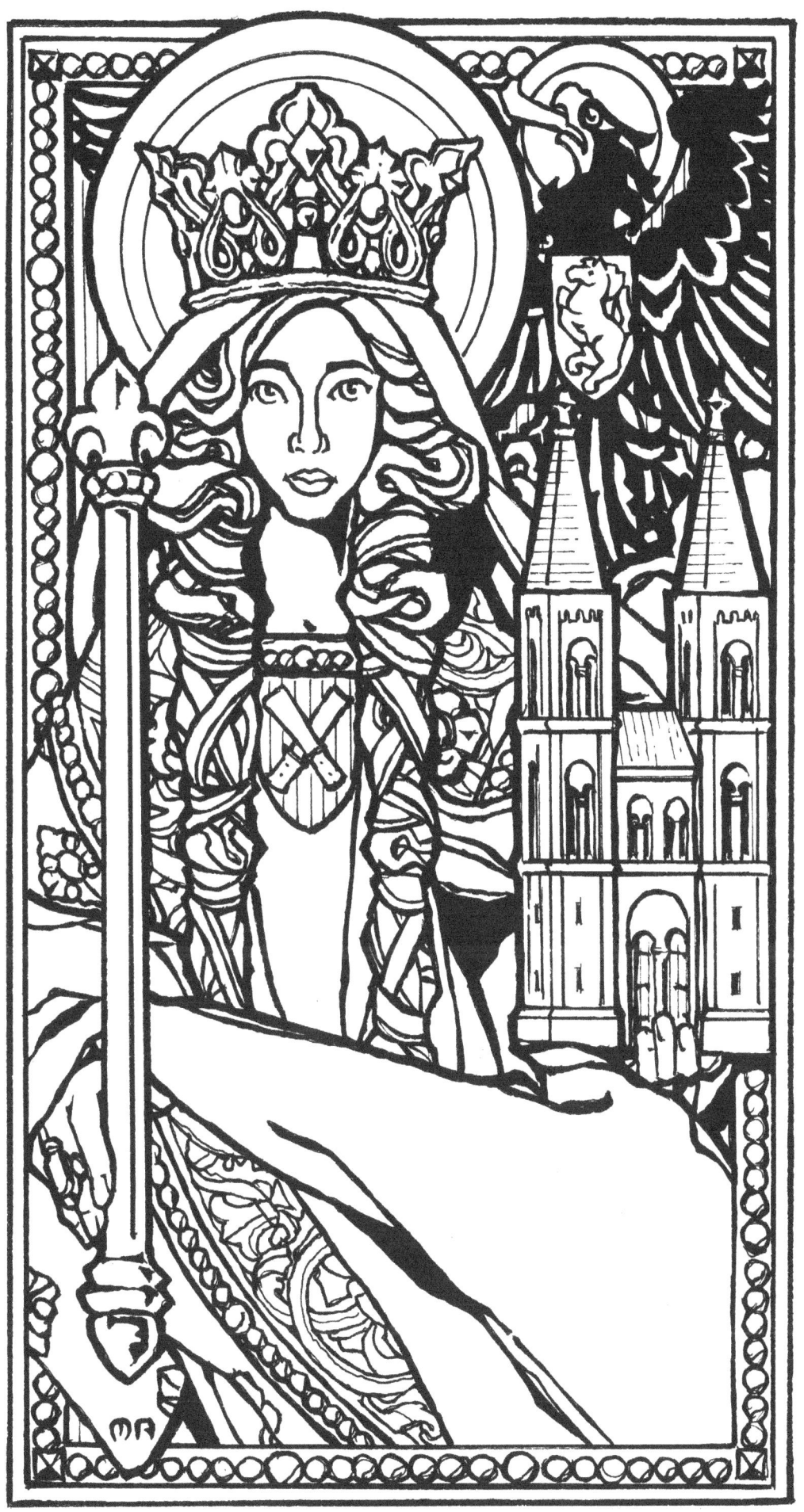

In this image of **St. Augustine,** the pear represents an episode from his youth, described in his *Confessions*, in which he and other boys stole pears from an orchard. The symbol of a burning heart, pierced by the arrow of divine love, represents his zeal and charity in the Faith and his love of God's word.

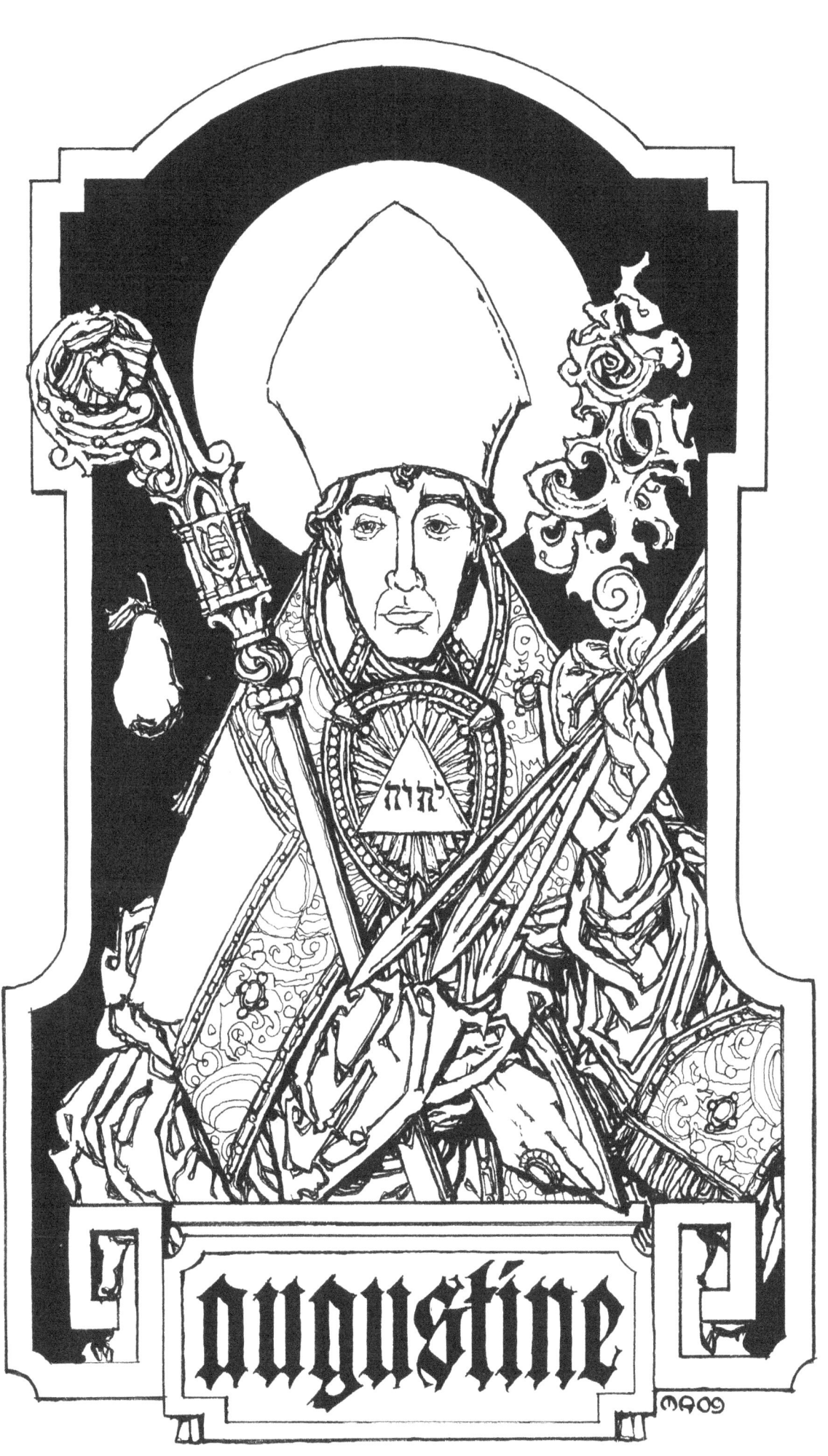

The Prophet Elijah is, like many of the holy men and women of the Old Testament, sometimes honored as a saint, particularly by the Order of Carmelites, who trace their lineage back to Mount Carmel in the Holy Land, where he was once a hermit. Their emblem can be seen at upper left, while the raven that miraculously brought him food can be seen at bottom right. His vision of a small cloud rising over the sea, described in the First Book of Kings, is considered to be a prophesy of the Virgin Mary.

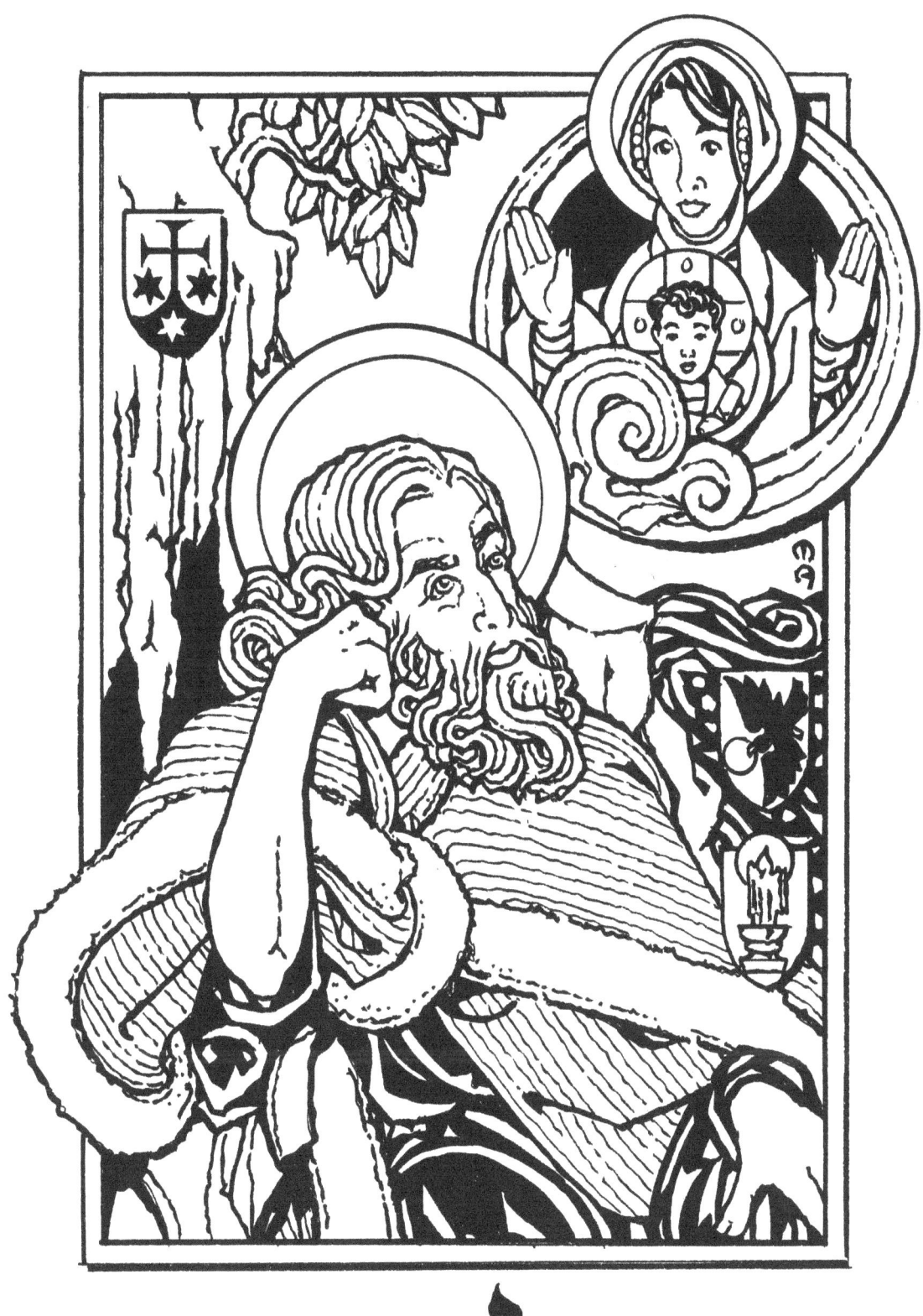

אֵלִיָּהוּ

St. Joan of Arc was a poor French peasant girl who at an early age began to hear the voices of St. Michael, St. Catherine and St. Margaret. These voices told her she must become a soldier and fight for France. With her help, many battles were won against the English, but she was captured by the Burgundians and sold to the English, who tried her for witchcraft and heresy and burned her at the stake in 1431.

Her legendary sword, found underneath the floor of a chapel dedicated to St. Catherine, is shown here, with its distinctive markings of five crosses on the blade.

Jhesus Maria

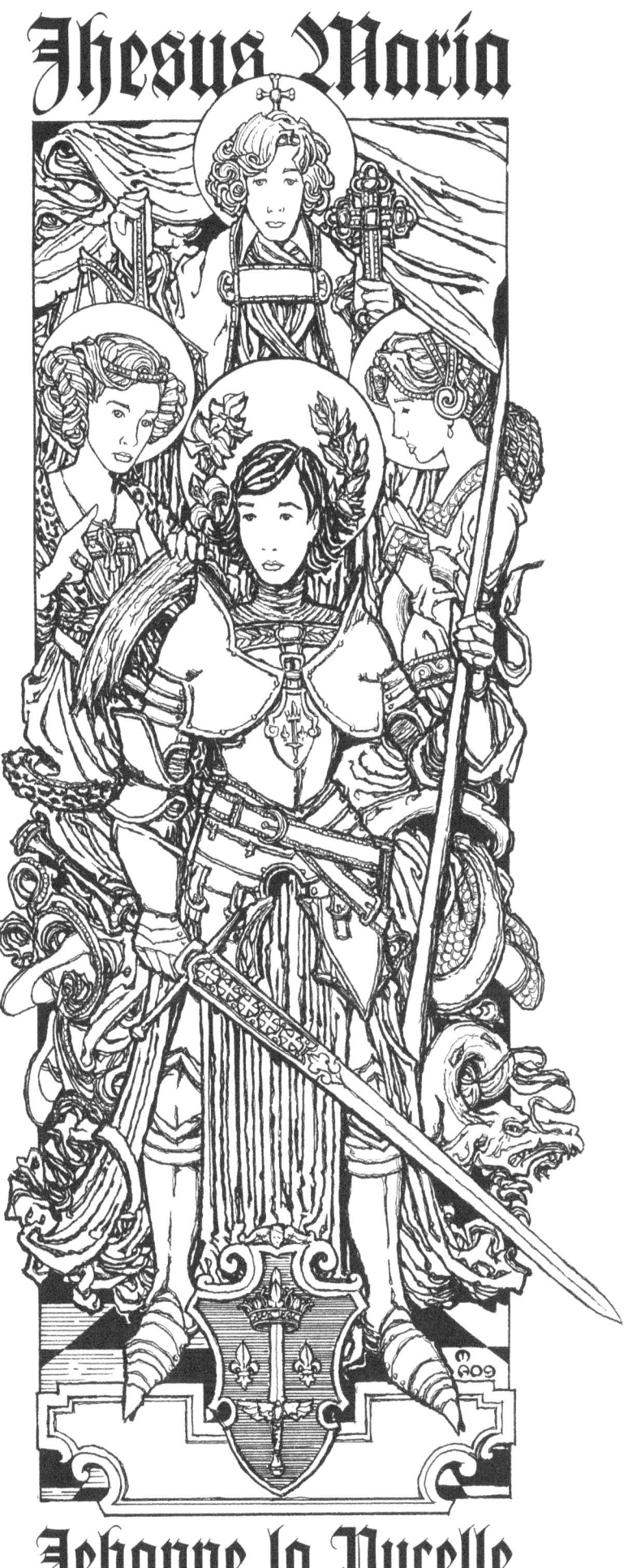

Jehanne la Pucelle

Our Lady of Grace is depicted in art with her arms outstretched, standing on a globe. She is surrounded here by symbols representing the Virgin Mary's various titles. The upper left is that of Mary as Gate of Heaven, while the ciborium (covered cup) and Ark of the Covenant recall her carrying Our Lord in her womb. The pomegranate decorating her robe-clasp is derived from symbols in the Temple of Jerusalem and represents both the suffering of Christ and—with its many seeds—the many members of the Church.

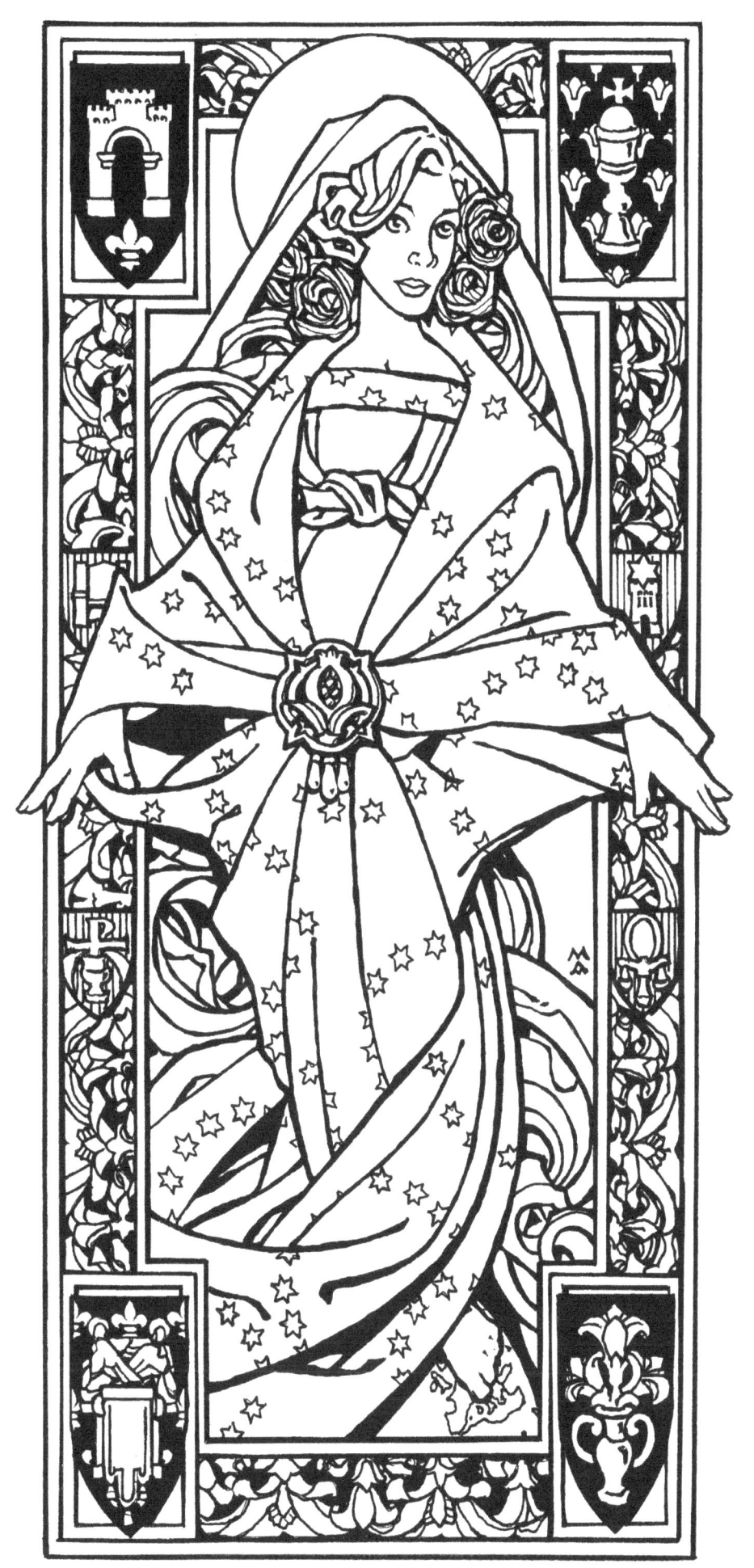

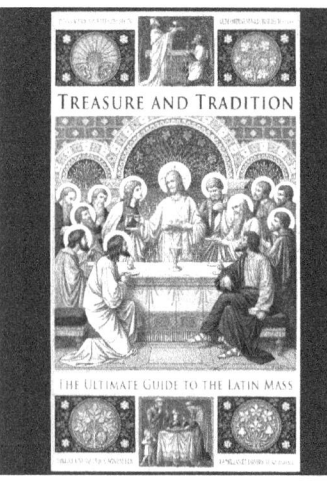
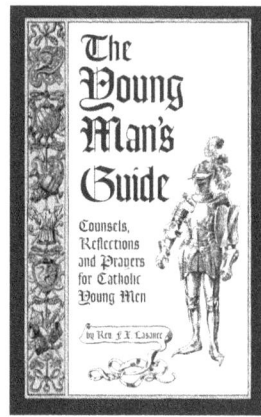
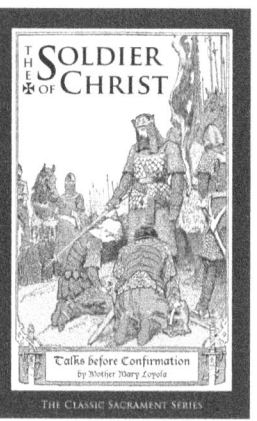
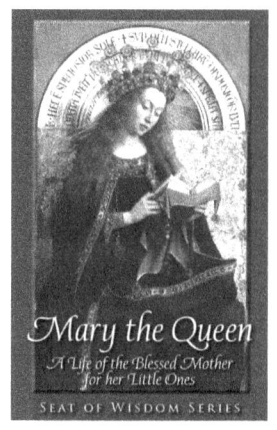

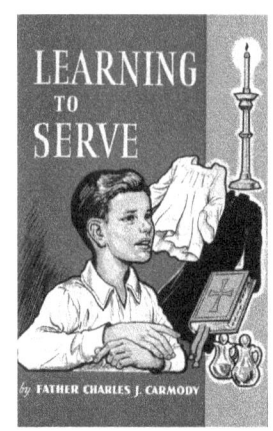
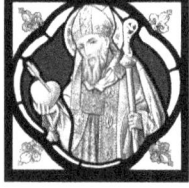

St. Augustine Academy Press

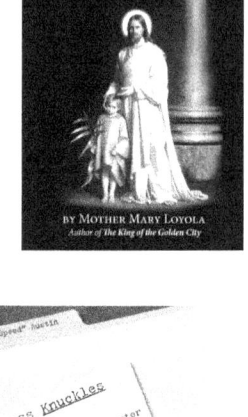

...because what children read really matters...

At St. Augustine Academy Press, we are dedicated to bringing you only solid Catholic literature from yesterday and today. To learn more, visit us online at

www.staapress.com

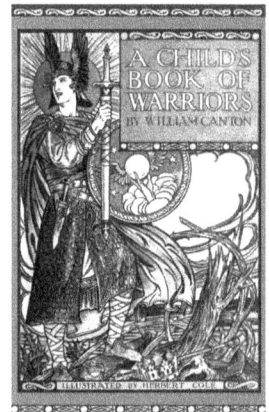
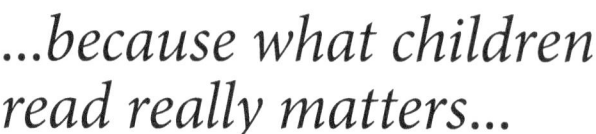
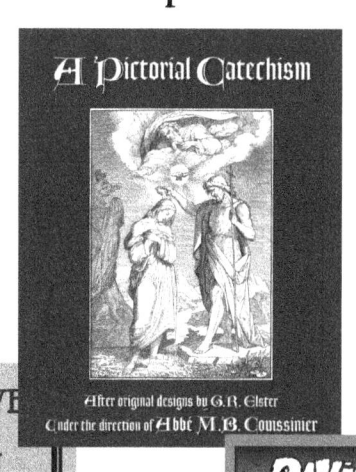
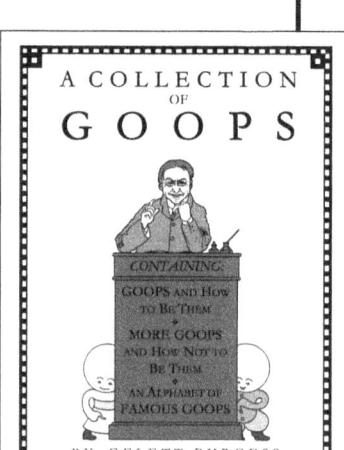
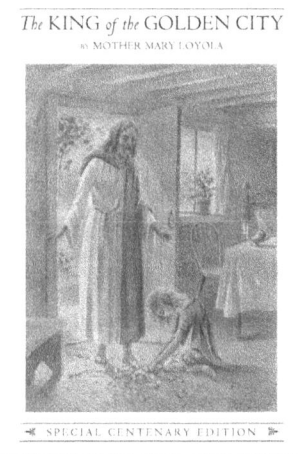
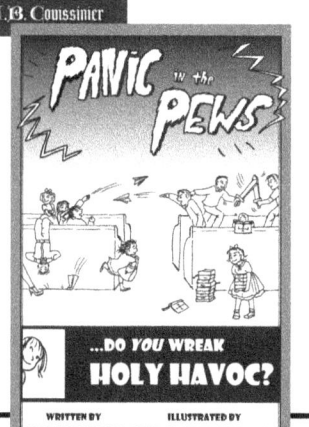

www.ingramcontent.com/pod-product-compliance
Lightning Source LLC
Chambersburg PA
CBHW040544220526
45473CB00016B/3017